Avenue J

The Road to Deconstruction

10-Day Devotional

Mission: To Proclaim Transformation and Truth
Publisher: Transformed Publishing, Cocoa, FL
Website: www.transformedpublishing.com
Email: transformedpublishing@gmail.com

All interior and accent images were retrieved by the publisher, via paid subscription / terms of use from Storyblocks. Author utilized personal ChatGBT subscription to organize his thoughts and generate related content when compiling this devotional.

Music in this book was Produced, Mixed, & Mastered by: Manny Vswrld.

Scriptures are taken from the Holy Bible, New International Version®, NIV® Copyright ©1973, 1978, 1984, 2011 by Biblica, Inc.® Used by permission. All rights reserved worldwide.

ISBN: 978-1-953241-65-8

Avenue J

The Road to Deconstruction
10-Day Devotional
Album Download

Christopher Sone Franklin

Dedication

To my kids, Ahlia and Christopher Junior—this is for you. I want you to know, no matter what life throws at you, you can always turn to God. He's got you, even when it feels like no one else does. And let me tell you this—your dad is strong, resilient, and I'll do whatever it takes to make sure you don't have to carry the same struggles I did. If you ever feel like you're stuck or going through something heavy, you can always come to me or your mom. We'll figure it out together. You're never alone, and we love you more than anything.

And to anyone who's scared to share their story—this is for you too. Your testimony matters. Your voice has power. To all the artists out there grinding and making music, I'm talking to you: you can do this. You can write, create, and even take it a step further. Pair your music with something bigger, like a devotional, something that hits people's souls and points them to God.

Making music is dope, but when you use it to inspire and make a real change? That's next level. Let's show the world what we're about. Keep pushing, keep creating, and let's make something that lasts.

Acknowledgement

First off, I gotta shout out my wife, Stephanie. Babe, you've been my rock through everything. We've been through some real tough times, but you never gave up on me. When I was struggling with anxiety and panic attacks, you were always there, reminding me to give it all to God. I honestly don't know where I'd be without you.

To my brother, Will—man, thank you for all those late-night calls, sometimes as early as two in the morning. No matter what time it was, you'd pick up and walk me through whatever I was dealing with. You didn't just listen—you showed up every single time. You're more than my brother—you're my lifeline when I need it the most.

To my mom, Violet—thank you for always being patient with me. I know I wasn't the easiest kid, with all my anxiety, nightmares, and OCD. I remember rearranging my room two or three times a month because everything had to feel "just right." You never made me feel weird about it—you just loved me through it.

And to my dad, Ray—I've got to be honest, there was a time when I was hurt because you left Jersey to go to Arizona. It wasn't easy for me back then, but since Ahlia was born, you've made up for all of that. You've been there for me in the ways that really mattered, helping me stay on my feet and making sure my family always had what we needed. You've reminded me of my wild childhood, my crazy antics, and the things I've carried with me. Thank you for showing up, for being there when it counted, and for being the dad I needed.

To my friends—you're the real ones. God really blessed me with a circle that keeps me inspired and motivated. You pushed me to write this book and kept me going with your ideas and encouragement. I couldn't have done this without you.

This book is my heart on paper, and it wouldn't exist without the love, support, and late-night conversations I've had with all of you. Thank you for believing in me. I love y'all.

Table of Contents

Introduction:
The Road to Deconstruction

Welcome to *Avenue J*, a collection of songs that trace the journey of Christopher Sone Franklin from darkness to light, from despair to hope, and from brokenness to redemption.

Christopher shares his deeply personal story of growing up in a turbulent environment marred by abuse, addiction, and trauma. Despite the darkness that threatened to consume him, Christopher found consolation in music and art, using his creative gifts as a means of expression and escape.

As Christopher recounts his journey, listeners join him on a spiritual odyssey through the depths of pain and suffering to the heights of faith and redemption. Each song in the album serves as a testament to God's faithfulness amidst life's trials and tribulations, addressing themes of anticipation, panic, pain, lust, fear, and resilience.

Through heartfelt lyrics and soul-stirring melodies, Christopher invites listeners to join him on the open road of faith, where each step brings them closer to the promise of healing, renewal, and reconstruction.

As the album unfolds, a newfound resolve is released for people to join Christopher by making their own journey of redemption, trusting in God's unfailing love and mercy to guide them through every twist and turn of life.

With *Avenue J*, Christopher Sone Franklin invites listeners to embark on an interactive journey of faith, hope, and renewal. May this 10-Day Devotional and album serve as sources of inspiration and encouragement to all who seek to find light when plagued by darkness and hope in the face of adversity. Each day includes a short devotional reflection, followed by a time of prayer, and personal reflection. This devotional journey offers readers the opportunity to connect with God's Word and find encouragement in Christopher's testimony proving God's faithfulness.

Testimonies

Christopher's Testimony

I am Christopher Sone Franklin, born and raised in Jersey City, New Jersey. My life has been one filled with challenges and unforgettable encounters with God.

When I was young, I witnessed my mother being abused by a woman she was in a relationship with all of my childhood and a man who later got her hooked to crack cocaine and almost killed her. Combined with the absence of my father, she took the road of addiction that held my family captive. The stress and confusion drove me to write music and create art, yet I also delt with the trauma of molestation in secret that was inflicted upon me by those closest to me. My response to this pain was rebellion, which led me down a path of trouble and unfulfillment of my own.

I was given an ADHD diagnosis and prescribed Adderall. Still, my nights were haunted, filled with nightmares, and my days clouded by frustration and anger, with no relief.

Decades later in the depths of my brokenness, I encountered the saving grace of Jesus Christ. The miraculous revival of my daughter, whom I thought I lost to death, brought me to my knees in awe and gratitude. When my daughter Ahlia was five years old, she drowned in a pool, a mere three feet away from where I stood. My eyes locked onto her tiny body, lying lifeless at the bottom of the pool, and I dove in, pulling her limp form into my arms. As I sank to my knees, cradling my daughter's cold body, I begged God for a miracle. I had recently begun following Christ and clung to my faith in that desperate moment.

Her grandfather, with no prior experience in CPR, sprang into action and performed it on Ahlia. To my astonishment, he revived her without breaking a single rib. When the ambulance rushed her to a children's hospital in Tampa, the doctors marveled at her survival; she shouldn't have lived after being submerged for so long.

That day changed everything for me and my family, igniting a fire of devotion for Christ that continues to burn within me. I have followed Jesus from that moment on. I made a solemn vow to serve the Lord for the rest of my days, and to share His love through my music.

He led my family and me to Avenue J, where the process of deconstruction and reconstruction began. We lived in three different houses on this same block and in each house we lived, God revealed new facets of His grace and healing.

Breaking down layers of burdens through my albums: *A.R.T.*, *Illuminate*, *Dirty Laundry*, and *Extricated*, I poured out my heart to the Lord, thanking Him for His faithfulness, especially in trying times. Each song became a testament to God's transformative power, addressing themes of anticipation, panic, pain, lust, fear, and resilience. Now, I knew it was time to put it all in one Album, *Avenue J*.

Through it all, I learned to surrender to God's will, allowing Him to heal my wounds and order my steps. Today, as I reflect on my journey, I stand as a witness to God's never changing love and mercy. My life is a testament to His faithfulness, and I am committed to sharing His message of hope with the world. May my testimony inspire others to trust in God's plan for their lives and find strength in His enduring love.

Stephanie Franklin's Testimony

I'm beyond proud of my husband, Christopher. Watching him go through the process of writing *Avenue J* was nothing short of inspiring. It's one thing to know someone's story, but it's another to see them put their heart and soul on paper to share with the world. Christopher has been through so much, and I know the process of writing this book wasn't just therapeutic for him—it was a calling.

Seeing him pour his emotions, experiences, and lessons into every page made me reflect on our journey together. Since 2010, I've had the privilege of walking alongside him. I've seen how much he has changed for the better—not just as a man but as a husband, a father, and a servant of God.

This book didn't just challenge Christopher; it challenged us. There were moments when he was wrestling with his past, moments of vulnerability where he wasn't just writing words—he was reliving memories, some painful and some triumphant. And through it all, we leaned on each other.

We've faced hard battles as a couple, battles that could have broken us. But we've learned that when we keep building each other up, when we make Christ the foundation of our lives, there's nothing that can tear us apart. Writing *Avenue J* was a reminder of that. It reminded me of Christopher's resilience and his desire to be a light for others. It also reminded me of the strength God has given us as a couple.

I know this book will touch lives around the world, not just because of Christopher's story but because of the hope it carries. To see him transform his pain into purpose and his trials into testimony is a gift—not just to those who will read it but to me as his wife.

We've come out of this writing process stronger. Our marriage has grown deeper, and our faith has grown bolder. And I know that as long as we continue to build each other up, there's no battle we can't face together.

1: Anticipating
The Burden of Anticipation

Song Bio:

Anticipating, is a soul-stirring anthem encapsulating the journey of faith throughout life's trials and tribulations. With poignant lyrics and emotive melodies, the song navigates themes of fear, courage, and unwavering faith in the face of adversity.

Through verses that speak to the heart, the song captures the essence of walking in the light even when encroached by darkness, embodying the spirit of love and service even in times of hurt and struggle. It delves into the necessity of keeping faith alive, anchoring oneself in the word of God, and persisting in serving others with compassion.

The chorus resonates with a sense of anticipation, acknowledging the sacrifices and challenges of the journey while affirming its ultimate worth and significance. It encapsulates the resolve to persevere through the night season until day breaks.

Interwoven with metaphors and vivid imagery, the song encourages listeners to confront their fears, make courageous choices, and submit themselves to the Power greater than themselves. It speaks to the universal human experience of facing trials, seeking redemption, and finding comfort by embracing faith.

Anticipating, beckons listeners to respond to their divine calling, reminding them of the impending return of a Savior who will redeem and unite the righteous. It instills a sense of hope and purpose, urging individuals to hold steadfast to their beliefs and trust the power of faith.

Song Lyrics:

I know God is love
I know, I know it's scary where we're walking
We should be the light inside the darkness
Showing them their purpose
Handing out some love
We know they're hurting
Holding onto God
And keep on serving
His word is, there's life involved
We know to get Christ involved
The fight's not solved
We gotta keep His book in palm
We gotta keep our sights on God

Anticipating through the night
We know it's worth the sacrifice
We're trying to make it through the fight
But we can't be here when He smites

I gotta make a little choice right now
I know it seems foul
But man, I gotta cleanse my soul
I'm jumping off a cliff right now
I know it seems wild
But God is gonna guide my fall
Don't take it so literally

It's just a figure of speech
We gotta walk the valley
So we can reach the peak
We gotta go through trials
So we can feel defeat
We gotta give it to God
So we could . . .

Anticipating through the night
We know it's worth the sacrifice
We're trying to make it through the fight
But we can't be here when He smites

We got a date with our Savior
And He's coming to save us
Ain't no running away
Ain't no one taking your place
He's got an army of angels
All the righteous will rise up
Ain't no shrinking in shame
Ain't no one setting a date
He's gonna get right beside us
Ain't no time to divide us
And you know He's not biased
He will judge us the same
All this anticipation
Got us ranting and raving
Got our eyes off the Savior
Now we're lost in our sin . . . sin
When we get lost, we tend to run away
When we get lost, we tend to go astray

Anticipating through the night
We know it's worth the sacrifice
We're trying to make it through the fight
But we can't be here when He smites

We gotta make a little choice right now
I know it seems foul
But man, we gotta cleanse our souls
We're jumping off a cliff right now
I know it seems wild
But God is gonna guide our fall

Day 1: Anticipation

My life was filled with anticipation, always wondering what would come next. Yet, this constant anticipation led to overthinking and anxiety. Today, let's reflect on how often we anticipate the future, and how it affects our present. Let us surrender our worries to God, trusting in His plan for our lives.

Bible Verses for Reflection:

For our light and momentary troubles are achieving for us an eternal glory that far outweighs them all. So we fix our eyes not on what is seen, but on what is unseen, since what is seen is temporary, but what is unseen is eternal.

-2 Corinthians 4:17-18

I consider that our present sufferings are not worth comparing with the glory that will be revealed in us.

-Romans 8:18

Wait for the Lord; be strong and take heart and wait for the Lord.

-Psalm 27:14

Reflection:

Anticipating, captures the essence of the Christian journey, navigating life's trials with faith, courage, and an unshakable belief in the promises of God. The lyrics explore the challenges of walking in the light even when dark shadows linger and serving others with love and compassion even when it's not reciprocated.

As we reflect on these verses in the context of the song, we're reminded of the importance of keeping our eyes fixed on the eternal glory that awaits us, especially when faced with trials and strife. While we anticipate the return of our Savior and the ultimate fulfillment of God's promises, we're encouraged to wait patiently for the Lord, trusting in His timing and His plan for our lives.

The anticipation of Christ's return serves as a source of hope and motivation, inspiring us to persevere through the challenges of life with courage and determination. As we await His coming, we're called to live lives of purpose, service, and sacrifice sharing the love of God with others and remaining immovable in our faith.

Prayer:

Heavenly Father,

As we anticipate Your return and the manifestation of Your promises, grant us the capacity to persevere through life's trials and tribulations. Help us to fix our eyes on the eternal glory that awaits us, knowing that our present sufferings are temporary compared to the joy that will be revealed in us. Help us to serve others with love and compassion, and may our lives reflect the hope and assurance we have in You. Amen.

Action:

Take a moment to reflect on the anticipation of Christ's return and the manifestation of God's promises in your life. Consider how you can live with purpose and service, sharing the love of God with others and remaining solidified in your faith. Spend time in prayer, asking God for strategies to triumph through life's challenges and the willingness and ability to carry them out. When things seem delayed, still trust in His timing and His plan for your life. Reach out to a fellow believer or mentor for support and encouragement on your journey of faith. Remember, God is with you every step of the way.

Write:

_____

_____

_____

_____

_____

_____

_____

_____

_____

_____

_____

_____

_____

_____

_____

_____

_____

_____

_____

_____

_____

_____

Avenue J: The Road to Deconstruction

_____

_____

_____

_____

_____

_____

_____

_____

_____

_____

_____

_____

_____

_____

_____

_____

_____

_____

_____

_____

_____

_____

_____

_____

_____

_____

_____
_____
_____
_____
_____
_____
_____
_____
_____
_____
_____
_____
_____
_____
_____
_____
_____
_____
_____
_____
_____
_____
_____
_____
_____

2: Overthinking
Conquering Overthinking

Song Bio:

Overthinking, is a negative meditation on life's complexities and inner turmoil. With introspective lyrics and a haunting melody, the song dives deep into the depths of existential ponderings and the struggle to find clarity while feeling uncertainty as we search for meaning and purpose.

The verses explore the relentless cycle of thoughts that plague the mind, ranging from contemplations on life and death to the intricacies of daily existence. Bearing the weight of overanalyzing every decision, unsure of whether actions are right or wrong, helpful or futile.

Confronting internal turmoil, this song touches upon the sacrifices made in pursuit of creative expression and the toll it takes on personal relationships. Often, visionaries wrestle with the guilt of neglecting loved ones in favor of pursuing endeavors, questioning whether they possess the necessary resilience to endure the challenges they face.

Interspersed with moments of longing and remembrance, the song evokes a sense of nostalgia for lost connections and missed opportunities. It serves as a reminder of the fleeting nature of time and the importance of cherishing the present moment.

Yet, even in chaotic overthinking, there is a glimmer of hope and resilience. The chorus emphasizes that devastation can be turned to renovation, turning pain into growth and hardship into elevation. *Overthinking,* reflects often unmentioned common thoughts of discouragement and provides inspiration to break free from the shackles of our own mind.

Asking profound questions about trust, love, and the nature of existence, *Overthinking* invites listeners on a journey of introspection and self-discovery. It resonates with anyone who questions the complexities of their own thoughts and yearns for peace to replace the chaos in their thought life.

Song Lyrics:
I've been thinking
Overthinking
Way too long
I've been thinking of life
I've been thinking of death
I've been trying to patch
This huge hole in my chest
I've been thinking about
All the time that I have
What if it's less than I think?

I've been thinking so long
About all of these notes
Overthinking each step that I take
I don't know
If it's right or it's wrong
If it helps or it don't

Why is this
How I think?

I've been thinking about
All the time that I waste
When I'm writing these songs
All the time that it takes
From my wife and my kids
I wanna be great
But I don't think
I have what it takes

I've been thinking
Oh
I've been thinking
Overthinking
Way too long

I've been thinking
Oh
I've been thinking
Overthinking
Way too long

I've been thinking
Oh
I've been thinking
Overthinking
Way too long

Devastation
Turned into
Renovations
All of these
Conversations
Turned into
Elevation

Oh, I need
Motivation
Don't let me
Tip-toe around
My whole life
In these songs

Tell me about trust
Tell me about love
Tell me what's right
Tell me what's wrong
Tell me how it works
Tell me how I can get
Some peace
Of mind

Tell me how I had to suffer
When I was younger
I ain't have no
Other ways around
All of this trauma
And all of this trouble

Oh, tell me how I had to
Fight through this
All these nights through this
Ripping right through this
'Cause I
Was meant
I was meant for more
I was meant for life
I was meant to pour
I was meant to write
All these songs
I was meant to mend
All these wounds

I was meant to
Take all these shots for you
Take these rocks for you
I know
Why I'm here

I've been thinking
Oh
I've been thinking
Overthinking
Way too long

I've been thinking
Oh
I've been thinking
Overthinking
Way too long

I've been thinking of life
I've been thinking of death
I've been trying to patch
This huge hole in my chest
I've been thinking about
All the time that I have
What if it's less than I think?

I've been thinking
Oh
I've been thinking
Overthinking
For no reason

It's crazy if you think about it

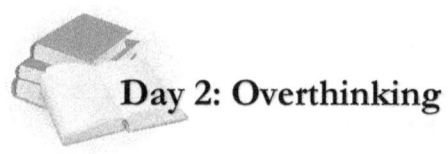

Day 2: Overthinking

Overthinking can consume our minds and lead us astray. An obsession with overthinking can cause us to lose focus and spiral into panic. Today, let's seek God's refuge in quieting our restless minds and finding peace in His presence.

Bible Verses for Reflection:

> Therefore do not worry about tomorrow, for tomorrow will worry about itself. Each day has enough trouble of its own.
>
> -Matthew 6:34

> Do not be anxious about anything, but in every situation, by prayer and petition, with thanksgiving, present your requests to God. And the peace of God, which transcends all understanding, will guard your hearts and your minds in Christ Jesus.
>
> -Philippians 4:6-7

> Cast your cares on the Lord and he will sustain you; he will never let the righteous be shaken.
>
> -Psalm 55:22

Reflection:

The lyrics of *Overthinking*, capture the relentless cycle of thoughts that plague the mind, causing anxiety and double mindedness about life's complexities. There is a mental tug-of-war between creative pursuit and the toll it takes on personal relationships.

As we reflect, through these verses, we're reminded of the importance of trusting in God's provision and seeking peace even with the chaos of overthinking. Just as I was longing for clarity and motivation to break free from the shackles of my own mind, I encourage you to turn over your anxieties and worries to God, knowing that He cares for us and provides sustenance for our souls.

Anxiety and overthinking can be overwhelming, but through prayer, faith, and reliance on God's promises, we are able to find the endurance necessary to face each day with courage and determination. This song serves as a reminder that the mind and emotions easily turn to chaos when they are not redirected and disciplined in line with God's word.

Prayer:

Heavenly Father,

In moments of overthinking and anxiety, we turn to You for peace and clarity. Help us to cast our burdens upon You and trust in Your provision to sustain us. Grant us the wisdom to navigate life's complexities and the courage to break free from the cycle of overthinking. May Your presence be our driving force through the uncertainties of life. Amen.

Action:

Take a moment to quiet your mind and center yourself in prayer. Surrender your anxieties and worries to God, trusting in His provision and care for you. Sort out your thoughts in writing to objectively process and release the weight of overthinking. Seek God as your perpetual help to gain understanding and clarity.

Write:

_____

_____

_____

_____

_____

_____

_____

_____

_____

_____

_____

_____

_____

_____

_____

_____

_____

_____

_____

_____

_____

_____

_____

_____

_____

_____

_____

_____

_____

_____
_____
_____
_____
_____
_____
_____
_____
_____
_____
_____
_____
_____
_____
_____
_____
_____
_____
_____
_____
_____
_____
_____
_____
_____
_____
_____

_____
_____
_____
_____
_____
_____
_____
_____
_____
_____
_____
_____
_____
_____
_____
_____
_____
_____
_____
_____
_____
_____
_____
_____
_____
_____
_____

3: Panic
Finding Peace Amid Panic

Song Bio:

Panic, is a raw and heartfelt expression which communicates the effects of mental health challenges, such as anxiety and post-traumatic stress disorder. Through its lyrics and soul-stirring melodies, the song exposes emotions related to panic and the desperate plea for relief, painting a vivid picture.

Panic, expresses overwhelming feelings coupled with racing thoughts and a frantic state of mind, articulating the feeling of drowning in a well, desperately gasping for air and seeking consolidation from chaos.

Throughout the song, there is a profound sense of longing for liberation from the bondage of anxiety and self-doubt provoking an intentional cry to Jesus, pleading for freedom from internal struggles and the torment of the mind. Glimmering past despair is a flame of hope found in sharing heartache with loved ones accelerating reconciliation. Through introspection and honesty, inner demons are confronted. and redemption is sought in the healing power of connection and spirituality.

The chorus echoes the dysfunctional cycle of panic and the overwhelming feeling of being alone in the struggle. Yet, there is a resilience that shines through, a determination to confront hurt and eliminate harassing thoughts.

Panic, resonates deeply with anyone who has experienced the paralyzing grip of anxiety and the quest for inner peace. It serves as a poignant reminder of the importance of reaching out for support, finding an immovable anchor in faith, and committing to transparency as a pathway to healing.

Song Lyrics:

I am
Suffocating
Barely breathing
On my own (x 2)

Panic
Always in a panic
Moving so frantic
Man, I need to
Breathe

Manage
Don't think I can manage
Feel like I'm
Drowning in a well

Breathing
Man, I'm
Barely breathing
When I start screaming
I need help

Jesus
Please come quickly
I need freedom
From myself
I get these thoughts inside my mind
They keep me panicking

Attacking every brain cell
Until I abandon all humanity
Reality turns into fantasy
Left inside this mess
Without no insight
Just some thoughts
Of discomplacency
Forcing me to think
The world is after me
Locking myself in my room
Until my wifey comes to rescue me
I'm a mess that needs some help, you see
My darkest days without no sympathy
All I need's a breath
Of symphonies

Breathing
Oh, I'm barely breathing
I can't keep fighting
On my own

Frantic
Oh, I am so panicked
I can't keep feeling
So alone

Reasons
Please give me a reason
Why this keeps happening
To my nerves?

Jesus, keep calling on Jesus
Guess some answers
Are unknown

I keep on thinking
All this pain was meant for me
Now why'd I have to be the one
To go through all this stuff so mentally?

I'm guessing
I'm the strongest in my family
But I got tons of weaknesses
So it still makes
No type of sense to me

I often wonder
How they took my innocence
So easily
Now was it me
That wanted some attention, me?
Now while I'm penciling these thoughts down
I start to ponder
Is there other human beings
Going through this mess like me?

And then it dawns on me
That Jesus was protecting me
From death
So I can write this testimony
For humanity

I'm managing
To keep it together
When sharing these
Darkest secrets
With my family

It seems I'm good
But honestly
I have no energy
And when I'm up on stage
I wanna run away
From everything

I'm wrestling
With all this trauma
That keeps haunting me
I've had enough

I just wanna seek God
Before anything

Panic
Always in a panic
Moving so frantic
Man, I need to
Breathe

Manage
Don't think I can manage
Feelin' like I'm
Drowning in a well

Breathing
Man, I'm
Barely breathing
When I start screaming
I need help

Jesus
Please come quickly
I need freedom
From myself

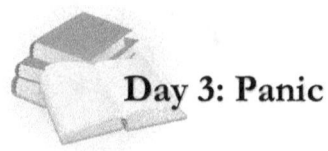

Day 3: Panic

Panic invaded my heart, depositing fear and hopelessness. Nevertheless, through my struggles, I learned to allow God to be God and to get *myself* out of the way. Today, let's pray for God's peace to calm our anxious hearts and trust in His inexhaustible love to carry us through every storm.

Bible Verses for Reflection:

> Do not be anxious about anything, but in every situation, by prayer and petition, with thanksgiving, present your requests to God. And the peace of God, which transcends all understanding, will guard your hearts and your minds in Christ Jesus.
>
> -Philippians 4:6-7

> "Come to me, all you who are weary and burdened, and I will give you rest. Take my yoke upon you and learn from me, for I am gentle and humble in heart, and you will find rest for your souls. For my yoke is easy and my burden is light."
>
> -Matthew 11:28-30

> The righteous cry out, and the Lord hears them; he delivers them from all their troubles. The Lord is close to the brokenhearted and saves those who are crushed in spirit.
>
> -Psalm 34:17-18

Reflection:

The lyrics of *Panic* vividly depict the relentless grip of anxiety and the desperate plea for relief. Regardless of feeling overwhelmed and frantic, I have found Jesus to be more than able to receive the burdens I willingly surrender.

As we reflect on these verses in the context of the song, we're reminded of the promise of God's presence and the peace that surpasses all understanding. Just as I called out to Jesus for freedom from my internal pain, I encourage you to cast your anxieties upon Him and find rest for your soul.

Anxiety can be paralyzing, but through prayer, faith, and seeking support, Jesus' peace becomes our reality. This song is another witness that we're not alone in times of difficulty and God is ever ready to provide comfort and companionship in times of need.

Prayer:

Dear God,

In moments of panic and anxiety, we turn to You for peace and strength. Help us to cast our burdens upon You and trust in Your promise to provide rest for our weary souls. Grant us the courage to reach out for support and the faith to believe in Your never-failing love and presence. May Your peace, which transcends all understanding, guard our hearts and minds in Christ Jesus. Amen.

Action:

Take a moment to breathe deeply and center yourself in prayer. Surrender your anxieties and fears to God, trusting in His provision and care. Confide in honorable counsel to better manage panic. The Bible tells us when Jesus cast out the *mute* spirit the people marveled. Help is often closer than we think.

Write:

_____
_____
_____
_____
_____
_____
_____
_____
_____
_____
_____
_____
_____
_____
_____
_____
_____
_____
_____
_____
_____
_____
_____
_____
_____
_____
_____
_____
_____

_____

_____

_____

_____

_____

_____

_____

_____

_____

_____

_____

_____

_____

_____

_____

_____

_____

_____

_____

_____

_____

_____

_____

_____

_____

_____

_____

4: Pain

The Power of Forgiveness

Song Bio:

The song, *Pain*, is anchored securely in the Biblical theme of forgiveness and redemption. In the narrative of the Bible, pain is a recurring motif, reflecting the brokenness and suffering experienced by humanity. Just as the psalmists cry out in anguish, the lyrics of *Pain* express the deep emotional turmoil and betrayal we often face.

The journey of forgiveness is central to the Christian faith, exemplified by Jesus Christ's ultimate sacrifice on the cross for the forgiveness of sins. We must intentionally process the complexities of forgiveness and acknowledge the deep wounds others may have inflicted upon us. When challenging intense pain and feelings of betrayal, there is a glimmer of hope that springs forth by faith.

The chorus echoes the message of forgiveness and acknowledges the need to release the burden of pain by extending grace to those who have wronged us, aligning with the Biblical principle of forgiveness as a necessary act that brings healing and restoration to both the forgiver and the forgiven.

The voice heard in the second verse of the song represents the divine presence of God, offering comfort, guidance, and reassurance available even in suffering. The power of forgiveness heals and ultimately leads to redemption. Draw from the never-ending supply of God's guaranteed love when you feel like you can't forgive.

In the Biblical narrative, pain is not the end of the story but rather a pathway to redemption and renewal. Believers find hope, healing, wholeness, and restoration through the redemptive work of Jesus Christ. *Pain* echoes the timeless message of reconciliation through Jesus Christ found in the pages of Scriptures.

Song Lyrics:
Pain
I forgive you for the times you
Put me through all this
Pain
I forgive you for the trauma
All the late nights with
Pain
I forgive you
For the times you
Forced me in that
Oof
Pain
Now I'm going through the
Motions
Trying to deal with all this

How do I address
The deepest, darkest pains?
The parts that kept me parted
From the love I wanna save

Man
My heart is on display
I wanna dissipate
From all this pain that I feel
My mind's in disarray
I'm feeling so betrayed
Revenge is served cold
I want a different plate
I heard that Jesus saves

But how do I apart?
How do I restart?
How do I forgive the ones that
Played a part?
How do I accept
That Jesus pardoned them
For all their sins
When the sins that they committed
Man, they're still not forgiven
By
Me?
It was so insane
Why'd they do this to my life?
Can they feel my pain?
Why'd they show me so much love
Then they hurt me?
Certainly
I know it's done in vain
They desert me
Unworthy
Is how I feel
Man, I'm introverted
Now I'm searching for a heart surgeon
Haaaa . . .
Why's it so ingrained?
Why's it so intense?

These memories keep coming back
Why's it so immense?

Someone teach me love
Someone rescue me
I want a different touch
While I'm dealing with this

Pain
I forgive you for the times you
Put me through all this
Pain
I forgive you for the trauma
All the late nights with
Pain
I forgive you
For the times you
Forced me in that
Oof
Pain
Now I'm going through the
Motions
Trying to deal with all this

I heard a voice
That silenced all the silence
All the violence
All the loudness
All the misconceptions
Told me, "Get up
'Cause the time is now
You gotta write it down
And don't be quiet any longer
Turn it up Sone
Open up the parts
Of your heart
Where it hurts the most
Let Me in

Let 'em out
Curtain closed
Forgiving them
Will help you heal
Maybe change their mind
If you don't
You'll hurt yourself
It only gets worse with time
Remember
They won't know love
Until they know Me
What greater love
To show them
Than to show Me
Homie?
So hold Me
And don't let go
I was always by your side
It's up to you to keep us strong
So don't you ever bat an eye
Anointed you from head to toe
Gifted you
With all the gifts
To keep you from the metronome
Protected you from the devil's blows
So let 'em hear the God you know
And rest and know
I sent an angel
And I healed you from all this"

Pain
I forgive you for the times you
Put me through all this
Pain
I forgive you for the trauma
All the late nights with

Pain
I forgive you
For the times you
Forced me in that
Oof
Pain
Now I'm going through the
Motions
Trying to deal with all this
Pain

Day 4: Pain

My journey of healing began with forgiveness. Undeterred by the pain of my past, I chose to forgive those who had hurt me, allowing God's grace to transform my heart. Today, let's reflect on the power of forgiveness in our own lives and seek God's help to unroot bitterness and display His mercy.

Bible Verses for Reflection:

Be kind and compassionate to one another, forgiving each other, just as in Christ God forgave you.

-Ephesians 4:32

For if you forgive other people when they sin against you, your heavenly Father will also forgive you. But if you do not forgive others their sins, your Father will not forgive your sins.

-Matthew 6:14-15

Bear with each other and forgive one another if any of you has a grievance against someone. Forgive as the Lord forgave you.

-Colossians 3:13

Reflection:

Despite the deep wounds and betrayal that I experienced and expressed in the lyrics of *Pain*; I found the ability to extend forgiveness to those who have wronged me. This echoes the Biblical teaching of forgiveness as an act of grace and compassion, mirroring God's forgiveness towards us.

God calls us to forgive others as He has forgiven us, I contemplated the complexity of forgiveness and its role in healing and restoration. The second verse showcases the omnipresence of Jesus Christ and reminds us of the importance of forgiveness as our prerequisite to healing and total peace.

Forgiveness is not easy, especially in the face of deep hurt and betrayal. Yet, as my song portrays, it is the imperative first step towards freedom. Through forgiveness, we not only release others from their wrong-doing but also find liberation from the chains of bitterness and resentment.

Prayer:

Dear God,

Thank You for the gift of forgiveness and the healing it brings. Help us to embody Your grace and compassion as we extend forgiveness to those who have wronged us. Empower us to release the burden of pain and resentment and fill our hearts with Your capability to extend forgiveness as a pathway to healing and recompense in our lives. Amen.

Action:

Take a moment to reflect on any unresolved pain or bitterness in your heart towards others. Pray for God's grace to extend forgiveness, releasing each burden to be made whole. Consider reaching out to those you need to forgive and seek support from a trusted friend or mentor as you journey towards forgiveness and healing.

Write:

_____

_____

_____

_____
_____
_____
_____
_____
_____
_____
_____
_____
_____
_____
_____
_____
_____
_____
_____
_____
_____
_____
_____
_____
_____
_____
_____
_____
_____
_____
_____
_____
_____

_____
_____
_____
_____
_____
_____
_____
_____
_____
_____
_____
_____
_____
_____
_____
_____
_____
_____
_____
_____
_____
_____
_____
_____
_____
_____
_____
_____
_____
_____

5: Lust

Breaking Free From Lust

Song Bio:

Lust, unmasks deceit present today which is parallel to Biblical narratives. Genuinely sharing, from personal experience, each line calls out the destructive nature of lust, human frailty, and susceptibility to temptation.

Biblical examples include King David and Samson, who were both enticed by the allure of lust and succumbed to its grasp, resulting in dire consequences.

The stronghold of lust enslaves and entangles individuals. The Apostle Paul, in his letters to several early Christian communities, gives a straightforward account of the struggle between the desires of the flesh and the spirit.

The lyrics illustrate utter destruction resulting from fulfilling lustful desires in contrast to the true deliverance and redemption of God available through repentance. Not only does God forgive, but full revival of the body, soul, and spirit are available in Jesus Christ.

The psalmists, in their cries for deliverance from sin and temptation, express confidence in God's ability to rescue and redeem them.

Ultimately, this song exemplifies the counterfeit craving of lust and the longing for spiritual renewal and transformation. Biblical strength and forgiveness, through faith in God, is still applicable today, to liberate people from the cunning spirit of lust, when we allow God's grace and fulfillment to replace ungodly lures. *Lust,* is a continual reminder that sin's desire is for us, but we have the power to rule over sin.

Song Lyrics:
I've been holding onto lust
Like it had no strings
I've been holding onto lust
Like it had no pain
I've been holding onto lust
Like it had no hold on me

I've been holding onto lust
Like it had no name
I've been holding onto lust
Like it had no brain
I've been holding onto lust
But the whole time
It's holding me

I've been holding onto lust
Like it had no face
I've been holding onto lust
Like it had no place
I've been holding onto lust
But the whole time
It's molding me

I've been holding onto lust
'Cause the things in my past
I've been holding onto lust
'Cause the pain that I had

54

I've been holding onto lust
But the whole time
It's killing me

I was
Fugazy
Fake to who made me
Lied to who loved me
Tried to keep frontin'
I wanted comfort
But all I needed was love

And it would
First tempt me
Then would torment me
Kept me on empty
Trapped me with envy
I wanted company
But what it left
Was lust

And I've been holding onto lust
Like it had no gains
Mama never told me
I would have to
Deal with these things
I've been trying to run away
But it keeps catching up to me

And I've been holding onto lust
Like I knew its game
'Cause Papa told me
I would never have to
Deal with these things
And I've been trying to forget it
But the memories

Are haunting me

And I was holding onto lust
'Cause I had no fear
I was holding onto lust
Like I had no care
I was holding onto lust
Praying God got a hold of me

Now I'm killing all my lust
'Cause it has no grasp
I ain't holding onto lust
Like the things of my past
I don't have to hold the lust
'Cause God got a hold of things

Day 5: Lust

Lust held me captive, feeding my shame and insecurities. But through God's strength, I found the courage to break free from its grip. Today, let's examine any lustful enticements and ask God to purify our hearts, and direct us away from temptation and towards His holiness.

Bible Verses for Reflection:

> No temptation has overtaken you except what is common to mankind. And God is faithful; he will not let you be tempted beyond what you can bear. But when you are tempted, he will also provide a way out so that you can endure it.
>
> -1 Corinthians 10:13
>
> Submit yourselves, then, to God. Resist the devil, and he will flee from you.
>
> -James 4:7
>
> For sin shall no longer be your master, because you are not under the law, but under grace.
>
> -Romans 6:14

Reflection:

Lust, shares God's promise to faithfully provide a way of escape in the face of temptation. Although what may be a stronghold for one person, may not be for another, most people find themselves entangled in various forms of temptation and sin at different stages of life.

These verses assure us that God provides a way out when we are tempted, empowering us to resist the grip of sin and find freedom in Him. Submitting to God's grace and operating in obedience to His spirit and not our flesh, frees us from the chains of lust and generates true liberation and lasting change.

Prayer:

Dear God,

Thank You for Your promise of deliverance and dominion to overcome temptation. Help us to recognize the hold that lust and other forms of sin may have in our lives and grant us the courage to turn to You for freedom and redemption. May Your grace empower us to resist temptation and walk in righteousness, knowing that we are loved and forgiven through Christ Jesus. Amen.

Action:

Take a moment to journal your reflections on the Bible verses provided and how they relate to life areas of temptation and lust you have faced or are currently confronting. Consider areas in your life where you may be holding onto sin and pray for God's counsel and be diligent to break free from its grip. Seek accountability and support from trusted friends or mentors as you journey towards spiritual renewal and lasting change.

Write:

_____

_____

_____

_____

_____

_____

_____

_____
_____
_____
_____
_____
_____
_____
_____
_____
_____
_____
_____
_____
_____
_____
_____
_____
_____
_____
_____
_____
_____
_____
_____
_____
_____
_____
_____
_____

_____
_____
_____
_____
_____
_____
_____
_____
_____
_____
_____
_____
_____
_____
_____
_____
_____
_____
_____
_____
_____
_____
_____
_____
_____
_____
_____

_____
_____
_____
_____
_____
_____
_____
_____
_____
_____
_____
_____
_____
_____
_____
_____
_____
_____
_____
_____
_____
_____
_____
_____
_____
_____
_____

6: Fearless
Courage in the Face of Fear

Song Bio:

Fearless, is a powerful anthem illustrating the complexities of faith, doubt, and the unyielding pursuit of truth. With thought-provoking lyrics and soul-stirring melodies, the song invites listeners on a journey of introspection and spiritual discovery.

The opening lines of the song uncover the vulnerability that exists beneath a projected image of fearlessness. This dichotomy demonstrates the warring spirits of inner turmoil and the outward appearance of confidence.

At first glance, it is usually impossible to determine who is wrestling with doubt and questioning their purpose and worthiness, or who is wondering, *If my faults and burdens became known, would I still be accepted and loved by others.* These timeless ponderings are found throughout Biblical narratives.

As the song progresses, a longing for understanding and assurance is sought to confront existential questions that plague the human spirit, seeking clarity and an escape from the fog of doubt.

Yet, through it all, there is an unwavering faith in God's presence and leading. The chorus echoes the all-consuming love and provision intertwined in the promise of God's enduring faithfulness during life's storms.

The song's title, *Fearless*, serves as a reminder of the courage and resilience found in upholding faith, regardless of doubt and uncertainty. It encourages listeners to confront their inner fears and insecurities with boldness and trust in God's eternal plan.

Ultimately, *Fearless* is a testament to the victory we have in faith and the enduring hope found in God. It resonates with anyone who has grappled with feeling uneasy while moving in obedience, offering a message of courage, perseverance, and spiritual renewal in the face of adversity.

Song Lyrics:
I can tell you I'm fearless
But sometimes I fake it
'Cause I'm scared inside my heart
And man, I can't face it
And I can scream, "Help me"
And hope that you'll make it
Or I can say (beep) this whole fake thought
And keep on creating

If you can see beneath the surface
Would you still love me
Even though I'm hurting?
Would you still love me
If you knew I doubt
A lot?
If you knew that I still had some burdens?

Would you still love me
If you knew that I was wrestling
With all this mentally?

I'm pressing through
But honestly
I wanna know
What's on the other end?
Understand
I'm a man of faith
But I have questions
And only God can answer them
And is it certain
That you would love me
If I felt no purpose?
Would you still love me
If I felt so worthless?
Would you still love me
If I told you I
When I tell you I'm

I can tell you I'm fearless
But sometimes I fake it
'Cause I'm scared inside my heart
And man, I can't face it
And I can scream, "Help me"
And hope that you'll make it
Or I can say (beep) this whole fake thought
And keep on creating

If you can see beneath the fog
Beneath the mist
Would you still love me?
If you can see beyond the lies
Beyond the myths
Would you still trust me?

'Cause God did
And God does
And God knows

Who I was
And God said
That I will
Make it through
This storm

I can tell you I'm fearless
But sometimes I fake it
'Cause I'm scared inside my heart
And man, I can't face it
And I can scream, "Help me"
And hope that you'll make it
Or I can say (beep) this whole fake thought
And keep on creating

Day 6: Fearless

The enemy rallies to immobilize us, so our purpose goes unfulfilled, by imposing the spirit of fear, to plague our journey and paralyze us. Yet, we must discover that true courage comes from trusting in God's promises. Today, let's confront our fears with faith, knowing that God is with us every step of the way, giving us strategies to overcome every obstacle.

Bible Verses for Reflection:

> So do not fear, for I am with you; do not be dismayed, for I am your God. I will strengthen you and help you; I will uphold you with my righteous right hand.
>
> -Isaiah 41:10
>
> I sought the Lord, and he answered me; he delivered me from all my fears.
>
> -Psalm 34:4
>
> For the Spirit God gave us does not make us timid, but gives us power, love and self-discipline.
>
> -2 Timothy 1:7

Reflection:

Fearless, examines the contrast between moments of fear and doubt, while exhibiting boldness. Manifesting a conscious awareness of God's constant companionship in our lives, is the key of confidence needed to override fear. Just as the psalmist sought the Lord and penned their testimony of deliverance from fear, so can we.

As we listen to *Fearless*, let's acknowledge our own moments of fear and uncertainty, recognizing that it's okay to feel vulnerable and to wrestle with doubt. Nevertheless, let's also remember that our faith in God gives us the ambition to face our fears head-on, knowing it's truly the Lord who is our confidence.

Prayer:

Dear God,

Thank You for Your constant presence and assurance in our lives. Help us to confront our fears and doubts with courage and trust in Your promises. Grant us the awareness of Your presence to victoriously navigate through life's uncertainties. May Your everlasting love and faithfulness overtake us. Amen.

Action:

Journal your responses to the Bible verses provided. Describe how they resonate with your own experiences of fear and doubt. Consider moments when you have felt God's tangible presence during times of uncertainty and reflect on how you can cultivate a deeper sense of courage and trust in God's promises for your life.

Write:

_____

_____

_____

_____

_____

_____

_____
_____
_____
_____
_____
_____
_____
_____
_____
_____
_____
_____
_____
_____
_____
_____
_____
_____
_____
_____
_____
_____
_____
_____
_____
_____
_____
_____
_____
_____

_____
_____
_____
_____
_____
_____
_____
_____
_____
_____
_____
_____
_____
_____
_____
_____
_____
_____
_____
_____
_____
_____
_____
_____
_____
_____
_____
_____
_____
_____
_____

7: Menace

Embracing Our Uniqueness

Song Bio:

Menace, is a bold and introspective anthem that challenges societal perceptions and stereotypes, while also affirming our great need to operate in faith solidifying our identity in Christ. With dynamic lyrics and a compelling beat, the song invites each listener to confront preconceived notions and welcome the complexity of individuality.

The opening lines of the song confront the label of 'menace' often used when passing judgment and voicing misconceptions. The power of faith works regardless of adversity. God is on our side and fuels our energy to pursue purpose.

Drawing upon Biblical backing, the song echoes the theme of supernatural protection and instruction, even under societal scrutiny. Like David facing Goliath, we must learn to boldly assert our God-given identity and refuse to conform to society's expectations, trusting in God's providence to navigate through life's challenges.

As the song progresses, we get a glimpse into self-discovery and faith through recounted moments of introspection and wonder. Gazing at the beauty of the world, it is humbling to contemplate our place within it. Even while receiving love, conflict can be provoked.

The second verse asserts the need for balancing talents and abilities while reaffirming an ultimate commitment to faith. We also must refuse to compromise our beliefs or conform to societal norms, and instead relate our identities as followers of God, not faltering under pressure to alter our position.

Ultimately, *Menace* is a testament to the resilience and courage found in staying true to one's convictions and faith, even when it is difficult. Be challenged to examine your own perceptions and biases and offer a message of hope and empowerment to encourage others to embrace individuality and faith.

Song Lyrics:
I took a trip outside of my mind
So I can see what this world can be
Ha, yeah
I took a gaze up at that moon
I wondered if the stars stared at me
Do they?
I gain a lot of love when I write
But I also caused a lot of fights
I don't think I'm ready for their ways
You know why?
'Cause I'm a

Menace
Is that what you see?
Tell me what you think
When you look at me
He's a menace
I hear it all the time

God is on my side
He's my energy
Tell me what you want from me
I can't be what you want me to be
He's a menace
I can feel your vibes
Please don't waste my time

'Cause I can rap like it's going out of style
But the style never mattered to me
Haha, yeah
And I can write like a novel gets wrote
But this book don't need a beat
Ha, nah
And I can think outside of the box
And I can give you some hope if you want
But one thing I can't do
Is change my faith
Ha, yeah
You wanna know why?
'Cause I'm a

Menace
Is that what you see?
Tell me what you think
When you look at me
He's a menace
I hear it all the time
God is on my side
He's my energy
Tell me what you want from me
I can't be what you want me to be
He's a menace
I can feel your vibes
Please don't waste my time

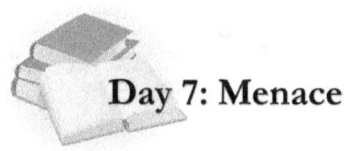

Day 7: Menace

I adopted my identity as a 'menace', refusing to conform to society's expectations. We must be bold and celebrate the unique gifts and talents God has given each of us. Today, let's embody our differences and use them to glorify God, knowing that He created us to shine our light brightly in the world.

Bible Verses for Reflection:

> But the Lord said to Samuel, "Do not look at his appearance or at the height of his stature, because I have rejected him. For the Lord sees not as man sees; for man looks at the outward appearance, but the Lord looks at the heart."
>
> -1 Samuel 16:7

> Do not conform to the pattern of this world, but be transformed by the renewing of your mind. Then you will be able to test and approve what God's will is—his good, pleasing and perfect will.
>
> -Romans 12:2

> I praise you because I am fearfully and wonderfully made; your works are wonderful, I know that full well.
>
> -Psalm 139:14

Reflection:

Consider how these verses relate to the message of *Menace*. Like the song says, we often confront societal perceptions and stereotypes; face judgment; and can be misunderstood by others based on outward appearances or labels. However, these verses remind us that God sees beyond surface-level judgments and values the uniqueness and complexity of everyone.

As we listen to *Menace*, let's challenge ourselves to champion our own uniqueness and identity, regardless of societal expectations or pressures to conform. Let's draw from the well of our faith in God and trust in His design and acceptance. Let's also strive to view others through God's perspective, recognizing the inherent value and dignity in each person, without any preconceived notions or labels.

Prayer:

Dear God,

Thank You for creating us in Your image, fearfully and wonderfully made. Help us to see the purpose for our uniqueness and individuality, knowing that You see beyond surface-level judgments and value the depths of our hearts. Grant us the courage to stand firm in our faith and identity, even when faced with societal pressures to conform. May we extend grace and understanding to others, recognizing their inherent worth and dignity as Your beloved children. Amen.

Action:

Record how the Bible verses provided relate to your own experiences of confronting societal perceptions and stereotypes. Take time to meditate on the truth that you are fearfully and wonderfully made by God and list ways you can cultivate your uniqueness and identity with confidence and courage.

Write:

_____
_____
_____
_____
_____
_____
_____
_____
_____
_____
_____
_____
_____
_____
_____
_____
_____
_____
_____
_____
_____
_____
_____
_____
_____
_____

_____
_____
_____
_____
_____
_____
_____
_____
_____
_____
_____
_____
_____
_____
_____
_____
_____
_____
_____
_____
_____
_____
_____
_____
_____
_____
_____
_____
_____
_____

_____
_____
_____
_____
_____
_____
_____
_____
_____
_____
_____
_____
_____
_____
_____
_____
_____
_____
_____
_____
_____
_____
_____
_____
_____
_____
_____
_____
_____
_____
_____
_____
_____

8: Let It Go
Learning to Let Go

Song Bio:

Let It Go, emphasizes the importance of deliberately releasing pain and grief, to move forward on the journey of healing and wholeness. With heart-rending lyrics and soul-stirring melodies, the song shares Scriptural truths, offering help and hope to listeners navigating through their darkest moments.

The opening lines of the song explain the battle between feelings of isolation and loneliness, even in the presence of supportive friends and family. The enemy is cunning and layers blindfolds over our eyes until the suppression of light becomes unbearable, and we yearn for an escape without judgment or lectures.

Thankfully, God in His faithfulness, reaches down to offer comfort while reminding us to still seek purpose in pain, grief, and hurt. We are then able to extend His comfort to others.

As the song unfolds, it becomes evident that there are benefits to releasing our burdens and trusting in God's love and provision. The chorus serves as a powerful reminder to let go of the pain and sorrow that weighs heavy on our hearts.

The verses echo the sentiment of shared suffering and resilience and offer empathy and encouragement to people facing similar challenges. They affirm the importance of reaching out for support and finding power in community.

Ultimately, *Let It Go*, serves as a beacon of hope, a lighthouse of direction to navigate the darkest of nights. God's agape love manifests comfort and consolation, building a spirit of resilience.

Song Lyrics:

I got some friends that check in
Every once in a while
And when I'm feeling low
Man, they always make me smile
Got some family that shows me love
But when I'm feeling down
I don't need no hugs
I get into this dark place
I need to escape
If you can relate
Just please don't be fake
I don't need a lecture
Or a lesson from you
I just need a friend
That can sit here and listen to me,
Man
So please don't judge me
These thoughts are dark
You say to give it all up to God
He says to face them
I'm feeling stuck
I keep on running
They're catching up

I ain't fast enough
I reached maximum
That air hits my lungs

Then they open up
I hear hope's around
I feel like giving up
Then God comes down
And He shows me love
He said son
I gave you all these feelings for a reason
So you can go help the ones that are grieving
I know it hurts
But let Me help you with the healing
Just know I see you
When you're going through your seasons
I need you to go out
And show them why we need them
The way I love you
Is the way I love them
Even
But when it gets too hard to take
And you can't breathe in
I need you to

Let it go, let it go
I know you can't feel your heart right now
The pain's too loud
I see you frown
Your tears have you alone
Know you're not alone
Let it go, let it go
I know you can't feel your heart right now
The pain's too loud
I see you frown
Your tears have you alone
Just know you're not alone
Let it go

I'm trying to keep it sane
But can't find my smile

And when I'm at work
Everybody knows I'm down
I don't think I can take no more
It's a year since you're gone
And I still feel low

And I feel it
When you say that you can't take it
When you say that you won't make it
Make it out alright
But can you feel me?
When I say that I have faded
Now I say that I can't fake it
And I know that you can make it

Make a way

How am I supposed to cope
When I don't see you no more?
I'm tryin' to make it out the rubble
But I still feel low
And I don't think I'm gonna listen when you
When you . . . say

Let it go, let it go
I know you can't feel your heart right now
The pain's too loud
I see you frown
Your tears have you alone
Know you're not alone
Let it go, let it go
I know you can't feel your heart right now
The pain's too loud
I see you frown
Your tears have you alone
Just know you're not alone

 **Day 8: Let It Go**

My journey of healing required me to let go of the pain and sorrow desiring to suffocate me. We relieve the crushing pressure when we yield our burdens to God, trusting in His promise to carry us through every trial and tribulation. May we forever look to His unsearchable redemptive love to replenish us.

Bible Verses for Reflection:

> Cast your cares on the Lord and he will sustain you; he will never let the righteous be shaken.
>
> > -Psalm 55:22
>
> Cast all your anxiety on him because he cares for you.
>
> > -1 Peter 5:7
>
> So do not fear, for I am with you; do not be dismayed, for I am your God. I will strengthen you and help you; I will uphold you with my righteous right hand.
>
> > -Isaiah 41:10

Reflection:

Today, let's meditate on these verses and find relief from fear and anxiety in them. Just as I did in *Let It Go,* seek and find comfort in God's love and provision. Let's release our burdens and trust in God's care. Let's accept the invitation to let go of our fears and anxieties, knowing that God is ready to receive them and bring to maturity the fruits of the spirit. We succumb to imprisonment in our mind and emotions by our unwillingness to cast our cares as the Bible says.

Prayer:

Dear Lord,

Thank You for the assurance that we can cast all our cares upon You, knowing that You will sustain us. Help us to present our burdens and anxieties to You, trusting in Your love and provision. Grant us the courage to let go of the pain and sorrow that weigh heavy on our hearts, knowing that You are always with us, willing and ready to uphold us. Amen.

Action:

Take time today to reflect on the Bible verses provided. Consider journaling your thoughts and feelings as you meditate on God's promise to sustain and uphold you. God is readily available; He never slumbers or sleeps. He is an ever-present help in our time of need. He will never leave us or forsake us.

Write:

_____
_____
_____
_____
_____
_____
_____
_____
_____
_____
_____
_____

_____

_____

_____

_____

_____

_____

_____

_____

_____

_____

_____

_____

_____

_____

_____

_____

_____

_____

_____

_____

_____

_____

_____

_____

_____

_____

_____

_____

_____

_____

_____

9: Keep On

A Renewed Hope

Song Bio:

Keep On, is not just a song; it's the cornerstone of an entire album, serving as the catalyst for the creation of *Avenue J*. With its powerful lyrics and uplifting melody, this song embodies the spirit of perseverance, faith, and renewal that defines the totality of the album.

An illustration of life's journey, overpacked with experiences and challenges that have weighed heavily on our hearts and shoulders. Nevertheless, courage is found to travel a new path, seeking a lighter load and a brighter future, symbolizing the regenerating power of faith and the hope of new beginnings.

Drawing upon Biblical backing, the journey is equated to that of the Israelites wandering in the desert, seeking a promised land of abundance and prosperity. They recognize the need for spiritual direction and protection as they navigate through life's storms and obstacles.

The chorus serves as a rallying cry, declaring a renewed commitment to living a life led by faith and love for Christ. It amplifies the Biblical teachings of walking in righteousness and seeking God's will in all things.

The second verse expresses a desire for deeper significance and emphasizes the importance of living out the principles of the Bible in everyday life, challenging listeners to move beyond superficial displays of faith and develop a deeper, more authentic relationship with God.

Ultimately, *Open Road* sets the tone for the entire album, inspiring listeners to embark on their own spiritual journey of growth, redemption, and refreshment. It serves as a reminder that with faith on the forefront, there is no obstacle too great to overcome and no dream too far out of reach. As listeners journey through the tracks of *Avenue J*, they are encouraged to set forth on their open road ahead with courage, conviction, and unwavering faith.

Song Lyrics:
I've been packing all my life
To get started on this journey
The further that it got
Man, the luggage got too heavy
I needed a carry-on
So I could carry on
The world was like Jack Frost
I needed an Amazon
Ran through a bad storm
You know it ain't last long
Glad that it passed on
I'm sick of the sad songs
Trying to finish strong
It ain't easy as it should be
Now I'm looking forward
To what it could be
Cuz

There's an open road in front of me
I gotta new way of living life
I gotta keep on loving Christ
I gotta keep on, yeah
There's an open road in front of me
I gotta new way of living life
I gotta keep on loving Christ
I gotta keep on, yeah
And there's no way
No way, no way
No way you gonna break me down
There's no way
No way, no way
No way you gonna stop me now
There's no way
No way, no way
No way you gonna break me down
There's no way
No way, no way
No way you gonna stop me now
Yea

Cuz I'm packing some lethal verses
And no, I'm not talking rappin'
I'm talking about the Bible
It's time that we take some action
Pronouncing the life of Christ
Ain't no business or even fashion
The boasting we do online
Is gonna give us no earthly blessings
This journey is barely easy
We're gonna go through some crashes
The riches that we are seeking
Are only found up in heaven
I know it sounds crazy

But just give faith a chance
Just like you give life a chance
Cuz

There's an open road in front of me
I gotta new way of living life
I gotta keep on loving Christ
I gotta keep on, yeah
There's an open road in front of me
I gotta new way of living life
I gotta keep on loving Christ
I gotta keep on, yeah
And there's no way
No way, no way
No way you gonna break me down
There's no way
No way, no way
No way you gonna stop me now
There's no way
No way, no way
No way you gonna break me down
There's no way
No way, no way
No way you gonna stop me now
Yea

Day 9: Keep On

Bible Verses for Reflection:

> [B]ut those who hope in the Lord will renew their strength. They will soar on wings like eagles; they will run and not grow weary, they will walk and not be faint.
>
> -Isaiah 40:31
>
> I consider that our present sufferings are not worth comparing with the glory that will be revealed in us.
>
> -Romans 8:18
>
> I can do all this through him who gives me strength.
>
> -Philippians 4:13

Reflection:

Today, let's meditate on these verses and find encouragement in them. *Keep On,* summarizes my journey, aiming to edify others who too have faced undesired circumstances, as a reminder that our hope is in the Lord. Despite the difficulties we encounter, we can trust in God's promise to give us the endurance to persevere. Let's hold onto this hope and press on towards the goal that God has set before us.

Prayer:

Dear Lord,

Thank You for being our hope and renewing our strength. Help us to remember Your promises when we face challenges and struggles along the journey of life. Grant us the courage to keep pressing on, knowing that You are always with us, and are the source of all we need. Amen.

Action:

Take sometime today to reflect on the Bible verses provided. Journal how they apply to your own journey of faith. Take comfort in the realization that God is with you every step of the way, supplying all things needed for life and godliness.

Write:

_____
_____
_____
_____
_____
_____
_____
_____
_____
_____
_____
_____
_____
_____
_____
_____
_____
_____
_____
_____
_____
_____
_____
_____

_____
_____
_____
_____
_____
_____
_____
_____
_____
_____
_____
_____
_____
_____
_____
_____
_____
_____
_____
_____
_____
_____
_____
_____
_____
_____
_____
_____
_____

_____
_____
_____
_____
_____
_____
_____
_____
_____
_____
_____
_____
_____
_____
_____
_____
_____
_____
_____
_____
_____
_____
_____
_____
_____
_____
_____
_____
_____
_____
_____
_____
_____

10: Conclusion

Embracing the Open Road

Every ending point becomes the starting point for the next stage of the journey. *Avenue J: The Road to Deconstruction*, is an ember intended to spark a blaze. The restoration we see through Christopher Sone Franklin's testimony and the power of God's redemptive love is available to all.

Christopher intentionally shared his personal reflections and elaborated on the themes explored in his music, in hope that you also will partake of faith, healing, and renewal more intimately with God, deconstructing and reconstructing as the Holy Spirit leads.

From the depths of pain and despair to the heights of anticipation and resilience, each day of this devotional has offered an opportunity to draw closer to God and find virtue in His enduring love. Come back to this devotion each month, allowing God to reveal more to you, and as an avenue to measure the amount of change and growth taking place in your life.

Christopher's testimony serves as a beacon of hope, mentoring us through the complexities of life and inspiring us to trust in God's plan for our lives. As we reflect on his journey from darkness to light, brokenness to redemption, we are reminded that God is faithful, even during our deepest struggles.

As we pursue the open road ahead, may we continue to surrender our fears, doubts, and insecurities to God, trusting that He will lead us safely home. May we find solace in the promise of His unfailing love and the acknowledgement of His presence with us every step of the way.

Together, let us walk this road of faith with courage, hope, and a steadfast trust in the God who holds our future in His hands. May *Avenue J* serve as a source of inspiration and encouragement to all who seek to find light as they walk through the shadow of death and hope in the face of despair.

As we journey onward, may we cling to the promise of God's redemption, knowing that His love will equip us to overcome and learn from every trial and tribulation we face. May we respond with gratitude, knowing that we are cherished, valued, and deeply loved by the One who created us. Amen.

Bible Verse for Reflection:

> I will instruct you and teach you in the way you should go; I will counsel you with my loving eye on you.
>
> -Psalm 32:8

Prayer:

Dear Heavenly Father,

Thank You for leading us on this journey of faith and renewal. As we conclude our time together, we ask for Your continued presence in our lives. Teach us to trust in Your unconditional love and to walk in obedience to Your will. In Jesus' name. Amen.

Action:

Take a moment to write down any fears, doubts, or insecurities you're holding onto. Surrender them to God in prayer, trusting that He will lead you safely on the open road ahead. Reflect on Psalm 32:8 throughout the day, reminding yourself of God's promise to guide you with His loving eye upon you.

Write:

_____
_____
_____
_____
_____
_____
_____
_____
_____
_____
_____
_____
_____
_____
_____
_____
_____
_____
_____
_____
_____

_____
_____
_____
_____
_____
_____
_____
_____
_____
_____
_____
_____
_____
_____
_____
_____
_____
_____
_____
_____
_____
_____
_____
_____
_____
_____
_____
_____
_____
_____
_____
_____

_____
_____
_____
_____
_____
_____
_____
_____
_____
_____
_____
_____
_____
_____
_____
_____
_____
_____
_____
_____
_____
_____
_____
_____
_____
_____
_____
_____
_____
_____
_____
_____
_____

Letter From Sone

Greetings,

This is Christopher Sone Franklin. I want to extend my deepest gratitude to each and every one of you for faithfully completing this 10-Day Devotional journey with me. It means the world to me that you took the time to engage with my reflections and prayers.

Sharing my story and delving into past wounds was not easy, but your support and willingness to journey alongside me gave me the motivation to press on. Through the process of writing this devotional, I found healing and freedom as God worked in my heart, touching areas I didn't even realize needed His touch. His grace has been truly transformative, steering me towards forgiveness and healing in ways I never imagined possible.

As I poured my heart and soul into these pages over the course of three years, I discovered a deeper connection with God and a renewed focus on what truly matters in life—family, faith, and selflessness. It's been a journey of transformation for me, and I pray that you've experienced a similar transformation as you've walked alongside me.

Looking ahead, I feel called to share my story on an even larger scale, perhaps through a documentary. My hope is that by sharing my experiences of facing trauma, trials, and heartbreak, others will find hope and inspiration in their own journeys.

Once again, thank you for being a part of this journey with me. May God bless each one of you abundantly, and may His love continue to guide and sustain us all.

With sincere gratitude and prayers,

Scan the QR Code below to follow Christoper on social media, find out more about current events, access music / videos, make a financial contribution to support community wide impact, & more.

Additional Journal Space

_____
_____
_____
_____
_____
_____
_____
_____
_____
_____
_____
_____
_____
_____
_____
_____
_____
_____
_____
_____
_____
_____
_____
_____
_____
_____
_____
_____

_____
_____
_____
_____
_____
_____
_____
_____
_____
_____
_____
_____
_____
_____
_____
_____
_____
_____
_____
_____
_____
_____
_____
_____
_____
_____
_____
_____
_____
_____

_____
_____
_____
_____
_____
_____
_____
_____
_____
_____
_____
_____
_____
_____
_____
_____
_____
_____
_____
_____
_____
_____
_____
_____
_____
_____
_____
_____

_____
_____
_____
_____
_____
_____
_____
_____
_____
_____
_____
_____
_____
_____
_____
_____
_____
_____
_____
_____
_____
_____
_____
_____
_____
_____
_____
_____

_____
_____
_____
_____
_____
_____
_____
_____
_____
_____
_____
_____
_____
_____
_____
_____
_____
_____
_____
_____
_____
_____
_____
_____
_____
_____
_____

_____
_____
_____
_____
_____
_____
_____
_____
_____
_____
_____
_____
_____
_____
_____
_____
_____
_____
_____
_____
_____
_____
_____
_____
_____
_____
_____

_____
_____
_____
_____
_____
_____
_____
_____
_____
_____
_____
_____
_____
_____
_____
_____
_____
_____
_____
_____
_____
_____
_____
_____
_____
_____
_____
_____
_____
_____

_____
_____
_____
_____
_____
_____
_____
_____
_____
_____
_____
_____
_____
_____
_____
_____
_____
_____
_____
_____
_____
_____
_____
_____
_____
_____
_____
_____
_____